What I Found

Damian Espinoza

BookLeaf
Publishing

India | USA | UK

Presentation by *BookLeaf Publishing*

Web: www.bookleafpub.com

E-mail: info@bookleafpub.com

ISBN: 978-93-5744-441-5

First edition 2022

DEDICATION

For Debbie and Sabas

PREFACE

I've always been a long-winded person. I ramble and meander my way through stories and poems. Even as I write this, I'm reiterating in my own mind: "keep it short and sweet... don't be too wordy." And would you look at that? Three sentences, over thirty words droning on about not droning on.

My poetry typically reflected this. I would jot down these lengthy and elaborate pieces of work out of a love of writing. Putting pen to paper and flowing endlessly was a reflection of my passion for the art of the written word. I was not so much in love with my words. On the contrary, like most writers, I feel, I am my own worst critic. Writers are also their own worst editors. So, like most writers, I didn't bother setting limits on myself. What was written is what was meant to be written, how it was meant to be written. It was all gospel.

I wanted to find a way to humble myself.
Verbose poems with flashy five and ten-dollar
words become tiresome not only to read but to
produce. I sought out a way to challenge myself.

It was the challenge that comes with writing in a
haiku format that I found equal parts
intimidating and alluring. The limitations on my
words made me selective and critical of every
syllable. Each word had this sense of increased
and dire significance. I discovered so much
about myself as well as the world around me and
how I could express it all in the most fine-tuned
and beautiful way. Where I was worried that I
would feel shackled, the opposite happened; I
never felt more liberated. What follows are the
best words I have and my journey as I found
them.

And Off She Went

Fly blue haired Angel

You've got a heaven to build

We'll wait for you here

Looking Up To You

Hole punched velvet sky

Shield your eyes stars so blinding

You still shine brighter

Stormy

Drops crash into glass

You prayed for rain forgetting...

With it, sadness came

Four Walls

Solace hard to find

Layers shed calm the inside

Rest easy riled mind

Unrequited

Heart far out of reach

Overlooked but not unseen

She'd mean more to me

Bully

Stand and watch me fall

I know you only came here

To give me a push

Dana de Noche

Moon beams bring your bloom

The ingrates gawk at the Art

Of petals floating

Up Late

"Come to bed," she said.

"We've got all night to plan for…

"The rest of our lives."

Grounded

Angel sleeps soundly

Do you fancy her new wings?

She clipped them herself

Metronome

Your endless echo

What keeps my heart on tempo

Song stuck on repeat

Wallflower

Bogged down by the beat

Besieged by these two left feet

I'll just watch you dance

Bound

You'll know it's her when

She unties you and gives you

Permission to breathe

Kismet

13

I wish I knew you

Before the stardust split us

Some light years apart

Ambrosia

A warm whipped cream clit

Parted lips melt in my mouth

Dessert worth the wait

You're free, Love

Grow wild flower child

Roots dug deep; winds spread her seeds

Smile wide flower child

De Harina

The egg breaking bliss

Of foil wrapped gifts before dawn

Keep that comal warm

Want Ads

Lonely caravan

Seeks skies, moon pies and new highs

Must love getting lost

Imbibe

18

A hcavy hand drank...

"This beer tastes like piss to me,"

She said between sips

Ballad

She strums my brain stem

Fingers stroking my senses

Hum me something sweet

Pedo

We're raising babies

To take rides from strangers if

Their vans have WiFi

Precious Cargo

Please handle with care

This world of fragile beings

Do not spin or tilt